JUNIOR JUDO

Book 1

JUNIOR JUDO

Book 1

by Mick Leigh, 5th Dan
British Judo Association

Photographs by Paul Keevil

W. Foulsham & Co. Ltd.
London · New York · Toronto · Cape Town · Sydney

W. Foulsham & Company Limited
Yeovil Road, Slough, Berkshire SL1 4JH

ISBN 0–572–01228–4

Filmset in Optima by Filmtype Services Limited,
Scarborough, North Yorkshire and printed by St
Edmundsbury Press Limited, Bury St Edmunds, Suffolk.

Contents

Introduction

I hope this book will provide a useful introduction to the many youngsters entering the exciting sport of judo.

Although you can learn a great deal about the sport from this book, you should always study judo under a qualified instructor who will tell you when you are ready to try particular throws and holds, will correct your mistakes, provide detailed individual instruction, and help you if you have problems.

Please remember that because I say something should be done in a certain way, this does not mean it is the only way. Perhaps it may not even be the best way for you. This is one reason why personal instruction in the sport is so important. You should ask your instructor if anything is not clear or if there is anything you do not understand.

Always start your judo sessions with warming up exercises. These will prepare your body for the more strenuous exercise of judo and greatly reduce the chance of injury.

I will be pleased to answer any written queries as long as a stamped addressed envelope is enclosed with your letter. You can write to me at 14 Black Dog Walk, Northgate, Crawley, Sussex.

Have a good time, enjoy your judo, and be safe!

MICK LEIGH

About the Contributors

Mick Leigh started Judo in 1955 at the London Judo Society. His first instructor was Ted Cribben, 1st dan and later Kenshiro Abe, 7th dan and Senta Yamada, 6th dan. In 1960 he joined the Renshuden, also in London, where he studied under Trevor Leggett, 7th dan, Saburo Matsushita, 5th dan, and Kisabura Watanabe, 5th dan.

He moved to Sussex in 1964, and in 1965 founded the Mid Sussex Judo Club, which has had many competition successes including men and women in British teams and squads. In 1977 he founded the Kin Ryu Judo Club.

He obtained his 1st dan in 1958, 2nd dan in 1961, 3rd dan in 1966, 4th dan in 1974 and 5th dan in 1980. He has represented Great Britain and England and was an Olympic reserve at middleweight in the 1964 Tokyo games. He has been a senior examiner for some years and gained his European Judo Union Referee's Certificate in 1978. He was made an Honorary National Coach of the British Judo Association in 1976. In 1979 he was elected to both the BJA Management Committee and the Refereeing Sub-Committee. In 1980 he transferred to the Coaching and Technical Sub-Committee and was made Chairman. He has been a professional coach since 1975 and has been teaching children since 1956.

Paul Keevil is a 1st dan. He started judo as a nine-year-old at Croydon and District Judo Society, and practised there until he was 11 years old. He moved to Sussex and stopped his judo for several years, starting again at the Mid Sussex Judo Club with Mick Leigh in 1972. He won the Southern Area Kyu Grade Welterweight Championship at Crystal Palace National Recreation Centre. He has competed in Belgium and Portugal and participated in the Dutch Open and Scandinavian Open Championships. He has represented the Southern Area on several occasions.

Steve Rooney contributed to the planning of the book. He started judo in 1971 with Mick Leigh at the Mid Sussex Judo Club, and has since won several medals. He is Chief Instructor and Committee member of the Niru Hatake Judo Club in Cuckfield, Sussex, and a qualified BJA Examiner.

Chapter 1

The History of Judo

Judo comes from Japan. It is a combat or fighting sport. Judo was founded by a Japanese man named Jigoro Kano. JUDO is composed of two Japanese words, JU meaning 'flexible' or 'supple' and DO meaning 'way'. Judo means, therefore, 'the flexible way'. A person who practises judo is known as a JUDOKA. Jigoro Kano had practised the old Japanese unarmed combat called JIU-JITSU and he decided to make a useful sport out of what was purely a way of fighting without weapons.

He founded the first judo club in 1882 with less than a dozen members. He called his club the Kodokan. The Kodokan is in Tokyo, Japan. Today millions of people all over the world practise judo and the sport is now included in the Olympic Games. At the Munich Olympic Games in 1972, Britain sent a team of six men, and three returned with medals. In the Montreal Olympic Games in 1976, Britain sent a team of five and two returned with medals. No other sport in Britain has been so successful over these two Olympic Games.

In the 1980 Moscow Olympics, Neil Adams won a silver medal in the under 71 kg category and Arthur Mapp a bronze in the open. In 1980, in the first Women's World Championships in New York, our ladies proved that they are amongst the best. Jane Bridge (under 48 kg) became Britain's first ever World Champion, and she was not the only success. Dawn Netherwood (under 56 kg) took a silver, and Briggette McCarthy (under 52 kg), Loretta Doyle (under 56 kg) and Avril Malley (under 72 kg) all won bronze medals.

In 1981 Neil Adams (under 78 kg) became our first ever Men's World Champion in Maastricht, Holland.

The second Women's World Championships, held in Paris in 1982 confirmed our place among the leading nations. Loretta Doyle (under 52 kg) and Karen Briggs (under 48 kg) both won gold medals and Diane Bell (under 56 kg) won a bronze.

Our international successes can continue if you practise hard, together with all the other members of your club. Remember fitness, stamina and strength are fairly easy to achieve. Courage can also be developed to a certain extent. Skill is the difficult factor. Many hours have to be spent developing your skill if you have any serious ambition as a competitor.

The first man to beat the Japanese in World Championships and Olympic Games was Anton Geesink, a Dutchman. Now several different countries have taken gold medals in Olympic and World Championships. Japan is having a harder time as judo standards throughout the world are rising, and Great Britain is a major international force in the sport.

Judo was brought to Britain by a Japanese called Gunzi Koizumi. He founded the first Judo Club in Europe, which was situated in London and called the Budokwai. Mr Koizumi died in 1965, but his club remains one of the most successful in the world.

The British Judo Association was formed in 1948. The Association organises judo in Great Britain and selects teams for European, World and Olympic Championships. The British Judo Association is a member of the European Judo Union, and the International Judo Federation. They are usually referred to as the BJA, EJU and IJF.

Because judo comes from Japan, certain customs come with it. Judo's international language is Japanese. All the throws and holds have Japanese names and all refereeing calls are in Japanese. This means that judo people from anywhere in the world can understand each other in judo terminology.

Chapter 2

Dress

The suit worn in judo is called a JUDOGI. There are some rules on how a judogi should fit. For instance, the jacket should cover the hips. The sleeves must come at least half way down between the elbow and the wrist. The trousers must come at least half way between the knee and the ankle. When the belt is tied there should be about 200 mm (8 inches) hanging from the knot at both ends. The sleeves and trousers should be very loose fitting.

Tying your Trousers

You should always tie your trousers by threading the cord through the loops on the trousers and tying securely with a single knot and a bow.

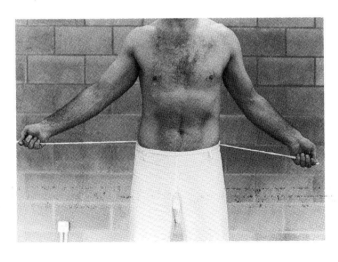

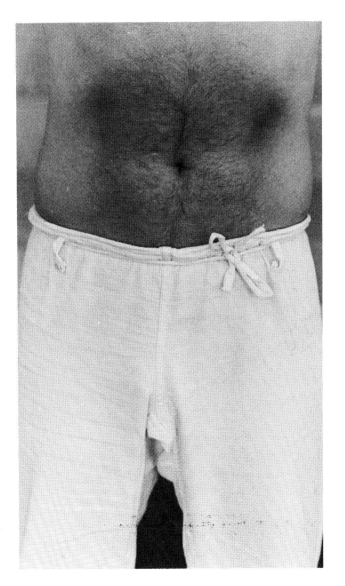

Tying your Belt

1. Wrap the belt around your waist and cross over at the back. The ends should be even in length.
2. Cross the ends over. Drop the top end so that it hangs loose.
3. Tuck the hanging end under the first loop.
4. Tie a square knot.
5. Tighten the knot. The hanging ends should be equal in length.

1

2

3

4

5

Folding and Tying your Judogi

There is a correct way to tie up your judogi if you do not use a holdall or bag. It is a very convenient way because you can then use the loop of belt to carry it over your shoulder.

1. Lay out the jacket as shown in the photograph. Place the trousers inside, folded in half.
2. Bring the lapels in to form a rectangle and fold both sleeves over.
3. Fold both sides into the middle.
4. Fold in half.
5. Double over.
6. Fold the belt in half and tie it round the judogi double so that you finish with a loop. This can be used to hang the judogi over your shoulder.

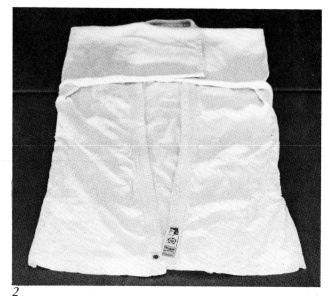

2

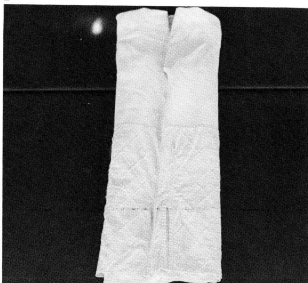

3

1

4

5

6

Chapter 3

Judo Manners

Safety

As judo is a combat sport it can be dangerous if misused, so remember to follow these few common sense rules for safety.

The DOJO, or judo hall, is the only place for judo demonstration. Never do, or show judo outside a judo club or class. Don't use your skill or strength to bully.

Be careful when you are near the edge of the mat, or TATAMI. You could slip off and land on a spectator. Watch out for other practising pairs, and make sure you don't crash into them.

Don't wear any hard objects, such as rings, earrings, hair clips, necklaces and so on. Keep your finger and toe nails short. Not only can you scratch people, but if your long nails get caught in your partner's costume you can tear your own nails back, which is very painful.

Always obey and respect your instructors.

Never chew gum or sweets on the mat; you may half swallow them and choke. It is wise to take dentures out for the same reason. Never practise with contact lenses in. They are very expensive and easy to lose if they come out.

Always sit or kneel properly and always face the action. You may have to get out of the way quickly.

Avoid talking during practice; you may bite your tongue when bumped or thrown.

Always warm up before practice so that your muscles are ready for action and are not strained by sudden or strenuous movement.

Correct sitting position

Correct kneeling position

Hygiene

This is really a part of safety. If you have verrucae or athlete's foot, do not practise without the permission of your doctor and your instructor.

Never walk on a mat with any sort of footwear, and never walk off a mat without footwear unless you have finished practising. This way the mat is kept clean. A dirty mat is a health hazard as the germs can get into your body if your skin is grazed or cut.

Your body must be clean for practice, particularly your feet. Your toe and finger nails should be checked before practice. They should be clean and not too long.

Your clothing should also be clean so make sure that your judo suit is regularly laundered.

Etiquette

This is a matter of judo manners. Some parts of etiquette were originally used because they involve safety. Sitting or kneeling properly is an example.

Remember we bow in judo because it is a Japanese custom and judo comes from Japan. The word for bow is REI. Whenever you bow you must always make sure your judo suit is tidy and your belt tied up properly.

You should do a standing bow when you walk onto your judo mat, and when you leave. You should also do a standing bow to your partner before and after your practice; also to your opponent, before and after your contest.

It is normal for a class to kneel on one side of the mat and the instructor on the other, facing the class, at the beginning and end of each lesson, for a kneeling bow. All bowing is a matter of courtesy or respect.

Standing bow

Kneeling bow

Chapter 4

Introducing Judo

The Three Parts of Judo

In judo, you are classified as a junior until your sixteenth birthday. You then become a senior. The main difference is that seniors are allowed to do necklocks and armlocks; juniors are not. Please note that this rule could change. In a judo contest your aim is to beat your opponent in one of two ways:

1. Throw them cleanly on their backs with impetus.
2. Hold them down on their back, with you on top, controlling them for 30 seconds. (You cannot hold someone down if you are between their legs. You must first escape from their legs and then hold them down.)

In both these cases, a full point is scored, and the contest won. Lesser scores are possible. For instance, a throw onto the back without sufficient impetus would be scored as a 'near point'. Two of these would equal a full point and win the contest. For this reason most people refer to a near point as a half point. A near point would be scored for a hold down from 25 and less than 30 seconds. Even smaller scores are possible, but your instructor will tell you about them when he (or she) considers you are ready. In all contests the referee uses Japanese calls to control the competitors. The most important of these words are listed on pages 25-27.

The word for contest is SHIAI (shee-eye). There is a winner and a loser. There is a time limit, and control is by a referee.

Contests are only one part of judo. The practice you normally have on club nights is called RANDORI (ran-door-ee). This is not a contest. You and your partner should use randori to improve your judo movements. You must try not to have stiff arms or crouch too much. Try as many throws as possible and move around the mat freely. Try to develop a throw on your left side (or your right side if you are left-handed). Practise hold downs from both sides, and practise going straight from throws into hold downs. If you are much better or stronger than your partner, you should handicap yourself, for instance by only trying left side throws, or only throws of a certain type.

There is a third method of judo training called KATA (karter). In kata, one person is always the attacker, and one the defender, or loser. The sequence of movements is fixed and the person being attacked does not resist, but gives the attacker the perfect chance for each technique. If practised often, and properly, you will soon be able to 'feel' the perfect chance when it comes in free practice or contest. You will be better able to take advantage of any chances your opponent gives you if you are trained in kata.

Gradings

When you do judo your skill and knowledge of the sport are shown by the colour of your belt and by the red tabs on one end. There are 18 junior grades which are called MONS. Mon means 'gateway', and the word is used because you are entering judo through the gateway of the junior grading system.

Seniors have a different grading system. There are nine KYU or 'learner' grades and ten DAN or 'teacher' grades.

Junior Grades

There are six belt colours in the junior grades, from white to brown. Mons are denoted by the red tabs on the belt.

Red tabs are only necessary on one end of the belt. The tab should go right round the belt. Tabs are 12 mm (½ inch) apart and 12 mm (½ inch) wide. They should be ribbon or tape and sewn on. Red ink or sticky tape is not correct.

1st Mon	White belt with one red tab
2nd Mon	White belt with two red tabs
3rd Mon	White belt with three red tabs
4th Mon	Yellow belt with one red tab
5th Mon	Yellow belt with two red tabs
6th Mon	Yellow belt with three red tabs
7th Mon	Orange belt with one red tab
8th Mon	Orange belt with two red tabs
9th Mon	Orange belt with three red tabs
10th Mon	Green belt with one red tab
11th Mon	Green belt with two red tabs
12th Mon	Green belt with three red tabs
13th Mon	Blue belt with one red tab
14th Mon	Blue belt with two red tabs
15th Mon	Blue belt with three red tabs
16th Mon	Brown belt with one red tab
17th Mon	Brown belt with two red tabs
18th Mon	Brown belt with three red tabs

On your sixteenth birthday, remove the red tabs from your belt. You will then be a provisional senior grade of the same colour belt you have. At the first senior grading you take the examiner will award you whatever grade he considers you are worth.

Senior Grades

The senior grades progress from a yellow belt to a brown belt for the kyu grades, which are numbered in reverse.

9th Kyu	Yellow belt
8th Kyu	Orange belt
7th Kyu	Orange belt
6th Kyu	Green belt
5th Kyu	Green belt
4th Kyu	Blue belt
3rd Kyu	Blue belt
2nd Kyu	Brown belt
1st Kyu	Brown belt

1st Dan	
2nd Dan	
3rd Dan	}Black belt
4th Dan	
5th Dan	

6th Dan	
7th Dan	}Red and white blocks on belt
8th Dan	
9th Dan	}Red belt
10th Dan	

Grip and Posture

This is the most basic way to grip in judo.

The feet should be about the same width apart as your shoulders. You must be relaxed and not stiff. The right hand grip uses the right hand on your opponent's lapel with your left hand on his sleeve under the elbow. If you wish to throw your partner by attacking his left side, reverse this grip.

Parts of a Throw

It is possible to divide a throw into three parts for the purpose of study. The first part is the breaking of balance or KUZUSHI (koo-zoo-shee). The second is the fitting of your body into position for the throw, or TSUKURI (soo-koo-ree). Finally, there is the throw itself, or KAKE (kar-kay). This does not mean the throw is done in three parts. The throw is one single continuous movement.

One of the main reasons throws fail is that the thrower fails to break the opponent's balance as he or she attacks. This leaves the opponent on balance and in full control of his or her body. If you come in for the throw (tsukuri) and then try to break balance and throw at the same time, you are not using the correct sequence. Remember – break balance, put your body in position, throw – kuzushi, tsukuri, kake. I again stress that the throw is done in one continuous movement. If you come in for a throw and your partner is off balance, he or she will be momentarily helpless and open to your attack.

Breakfalls

Breakfalls are known as UKEMI (oo-kee-mee). If you are going to move around a lot in randori you will get thrown quite a lot. You need to be able to fall without injury or pain. The most common method of falling safely is to slap the arm on the mat a fraction of a second before your body hits the mat. The arm, therefore, absorbs most of the shock of the fall, thereby preventing any injury. The thrower should help by giving support, usually by holding the sleeve.

The second way to fall painlessly is to roll. This is known as CHUGAERI (shoo-gair-ee). Your body should form as near a circle as possible. Your curved arm is held rigid and is part of the circle. Imagine your body is the rim of a wheel. If you put a wheel or hoop on flat ground it will fall over unless you give it a push. You give your body a push by driving hard off your leading leg. The photographs show two ways of doing a chugaeri or rolling breakfall, one using the other hand to support your weight. Remember to tuck your chin in. Your head must not touch the floor.

Reaping

The word GARI means reaping, and is usually done with the foot or leg. The action is similar to that of a man using a scythe or sickle to cut grass, and you cut your opponent's leg or foot out from under him/her. It is best to take your foot or leg past the point you are reaping and then bring it back. You can only block or pull if you place your leg or foot against your opponent's. In the same way you cannot punch someone if your fist is already in contact with them. You can only push – you need the gap to build up the speed and power. It is the same with the reaping or gari. Take your leg past the point you are going to reap and then bring it back. Ask your instructor to show you the action if you are in any doubt or have any problems.

Chapter 5

Contests

The aim of a contest, or shiai, is to beat your opponent by throwing him cleanly on his back or by holding him down on his back for 30 seconds.

A contest is controlled by a referee. At some contests, such as Area or National Championships, the referee has two judges to help him. They sit on chairs at diagonally opposite corners of the contest area while the referee moves around the area near the contestants.

Contest Rules

The rules of judo are not fixed for ever. They are constantly under review with the intention of improving them wherever possible. The latest contest rules can be obtained from the British Judo Association. Their current address is 16 Upper Woburn Place, London, WC1. They are very cheap and are important for anyone who is interested in competition or championship judo. You may also be able to obtain a copy from your club.

The three most important contest rules are:
1. You must not be passive. You must keep trying to beat your opponent and not just try to stop your opponent beating you.
2. You must both stay in the contest area.
3. You must not do anything against the spirit of judo.

There are also a number of things you must not do in contests, and some of these are listed in the next section.

Some Forbidden Acts During Contests

These are just some of the things you must not do during contests. Your instructor will explain any you do not understand, and tell you more if you are considered ready for them.

Many fouls are not written down in the rules as the list would be too long. These are the common sense things like biting, scratching, kicking, tickling, punching and so on. These fouls are all covered by point number six, 'any act against the spirit of judo'.

1. Pushing on your opponent's face with your hands, feet, arms or legs.
2. Dragging your opponent down for ground work.
3. Leaving the contest area.
4. Forcing your opponent out of the contest area.
5. Performing any act which may endanger your opponent.
6. Performing any act against the spirit of judo.
7. Disregarding the referee's instructions.
8. Holding inside your opponent's sleeve or trouser leg.
9. Holding the same side of your opponent's jacket with both hands for more than a few seconds (whilst standing).

10. Holding your opponent's belt for more than a few seconds (whilst standing).

11. Refusing to take hold of your opponent.

12. Adopting an excessively defensive posture (crouching).

13. Being passive.

14. Continually interlocking your fingers with your opponent's fingers.

Basic Contest Words and Referee Signals

All the referee's calls in a contest are in Japanese, so you must learn the correct words and signals which he will use.

Word	Meaning	Referee's signal
HAJIME	Begin	No referee signal
IPPON	Full point	Referee's arm ▷ straight up

MATTE   Stop   Referee's palm held towards timekeeper   OSAEKOMMI   Holding   Referee's arm forward, palm down

SONOMAMA	Do not move	No referee signal
SOREMADE	That is all	No referee signal
TOKETA	Holding broken	Referee's arm moved from side to side ▽

WAZA-ARI	Near point	Referee's arm out to the side ▽

YOSHI	Carry on	No referee signal

Chapter 6

Throws

Do not try any of the following throws until your instructor says you may. He will explain to you the best opportunities to successfully attack for the throws shown.

All the throws are explained and illustrated right-handed. If you are left-handed, change all the rights for lefts, and all the lefts for rights. An easy way to do this is to use a mirror to look at the pictures.

Tai-Otoshi

(Tie-oh-toshee)

Body Drop

Jump in or step round, so you face nearly the same way as your partner. Your legs should be spread and your lower rear right leg should be placed against the lower front of your partner's shin. Your left hand pulls round and your right hand drives up and over your right leg. Your right elbow should be down and your fist up. There is no hip or body contact. As you start moving into position you must bring your partner onto the toes of the leg you are attacking.

O-Soto-Gari

(Oh-soe-toe-gar-ee)

Major Outer Reaping

Step or jump forward with your left foot so it is a few centimetres to the side of your partner's right foot.

Your foot should form a straight line with your partner's two feet. Bring your right foot through the gap and into the air behind your partner. Point your toes and reap backwards against the back of your partner's upper leg. Don't put your foot on the ground, but swing it right through and up into the air. As your leg reaps and swings upwards, your head should go down. When you move in for the throw turn your head away from your partner. Try to prop your partner onto the heel of the leg you are reaping.

Ko-Uchi-Gari

(Koe-oochee-gar-ee)

Minor Inner Reaping

Draw your partner round to your left side, using his or her sleeve to pull on. As your partner steps forward with his or her right foot, slip your right leg between your partner's feet and reap back with the sole of your foot against the back of your partner's right heel. As you reap the foot, pull down with the hand holding the sleeve. Your right hip should be close in to your partner's stomach.

O-Uchi-Gari

(Oh-oochee-gar-ee)

Major Inner Reaping

Draw your partner round to your right side, using his or her lapel. As your partner steps round, slip your right leg between your partner's legs and reap back against his/her left leg. As you reap, pull down with the hand holding the lapel. Your foot should reap right round until it is behind you. Your right hip should be close in to your partner's stomach.

O-Goshi

(Oh-gosh-ee)

Major Hip

You must move in and turn so you are facing the same way as your partner. Your feet should be nearly together, in front of your partner's feet and pointing in the same direction as his or hers. Your knees must be bent. As you move in your right hand lets go and slips round your partner's waist. Pin your partner to you with your arms. Your hip must be pushed through past your partner's hip. Pull strongly with your left hand, straighten your legs and wheel your partner over your hip. Turn your face to your left.

Ippon Seoi-Nage

(Ippon-see-oh-ee-nag-ay)

Single Arm Shoulder Throw

Entry is as for o-goshi, but your hips must be square with your partner's hips. The right arm is driven under your partner's right armpit. Your knees must be deeply bent. Pin your partner to you. To throw, snap your hips back and up and take your head forward and down.

Ko-Soto-Gari

(Koe-soe-toe-gar-ee)

Minor Outer Reaping

Move round to your partner's right side, so you face his or her hip. Reap the right heel with the sole of your left foot in the direction your partner's toes are pointing. Pull down towards the ground with your left hand as you reap. As you move in try and take your partner onto the heel that you are attacking.

Tsuri-Komi-Goshi

(Sooree-komm-ee-gosh-ee)

Lifting Drawing Hip

Move in and turn so you are facing the same way as your partner. Your feet should be nearly together, in front of your partner's and pointing the same way. As you move in, use your arms to tilt your partner onto the toes of both feet. Your knees are bent and your hip pushed past your partner's hip. Your right elbow must be down and your fist up. Pin your partner to you. Straighten your knees and lift and pull your partner over your hip.

Chapter 7

Hold Downs

Do not try any of the following hold downs until your instructor says you can.

All the hold downs are explained and illustrated right-handed. If you are left-handed, change all the rights for lefts, and all the lefts for rights.

If you are in pain at any time and wish to submit or 'give in', tap your partner twice or more, or bang the mat twice or more with your arm or leg, or call out 'yes'. Always let go if someone submits.

Kesa-Gatame

(Kez-er-gat-armay)

Scarf Holding

1. Your hip must be in contact with your partner's side.

2. Your hips and head must be as low as possible.

3. Your partner's arm must be tightly trapped.

4. Your legs must be spread and the front leg should have the little toe on the ground.

Yoko-Shiho-Gatame

(Yoe-koe-shee-hoe-gatarmay)

Side Four Quarters

1. Your chest weight must be on your partner's chest.

2. One knee should be tightly against your partner's hip and your other leg straight, with the toes tucked under and the knee on the ground.

3. Your hips must be as low as possible.

4. Turn your face towards your partner's face and keep your chin in.

Kami-Shiho-Gatame

(Kammee-shee-hoe-gatarmay)

Upper Four Quarters

1. Your chest weight must be on your partner's chest.

2. Your hips must be as low as possible.

3. Your arms go under your partner's shoulders and grip the belt.

4. Your legs wide apart, toes tucked under, knees on the ground.

5. One side of your face should be on your partner's stomach, with your chin in.

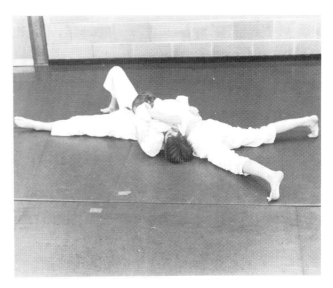

Tate-Shiho-Gatame

(Tar-tay-shee-hoe-gatarmay)

Lengthwise Four Quarters

1. Sit astride your partner's stomach and entwine your legs by taking them outwards and under your partner's. Lie along your partner's chest.

2. Trap an arm and wrap your right arm round your partner's neck. Grip the cloth with both hands. Your left hand holds your own right collar.

3. Keep your hips as low as possible.

4. Keep your forehead near the mat.

Kata-Gatame

(Karter-gatarmay)

Shoulder Holding

This hold down is very similar to kesa-gatame. The difference is in the trapping of your partner's arm. Instead of trapping it under your armpit, place it by your partner's right ear and trap it there with your head. Link your hands together in the 'butcher's hook' grip. Remember this can be a painful hold so don't squeeze too hard to start with. Just strongly enough to control is sufficient. Other major points are the same as kesa-gatame. There is another way to do kata-gatame. Ask your instructor to show you.

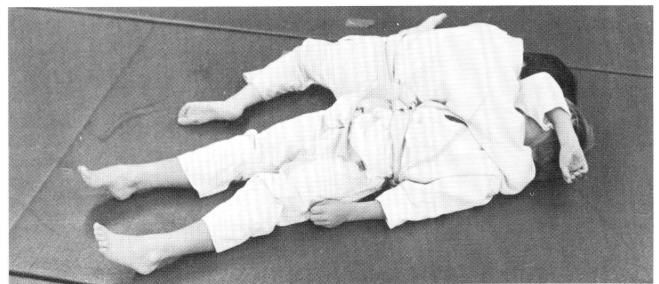

Mune-Gatame

(Moon-ee-gatarmay)

Chest Holding

1. This hold down is similar to yoko-shiho-gatame. Your chest weight must be on your partner's chest.

2. Keep your hips as low as possible.

3. One knee should be in at the hip and the other out straight, with the toes under.

4. The major difference between mune-gatame and yoko-shiho-gatame is in the use of your arms. Wrap them both round your partner's shoulder and grip the cloth.

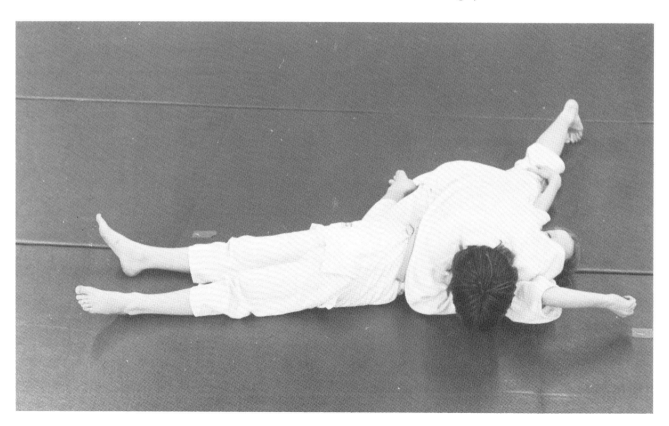

Questionnaire

If you have read this book carefully, you should know the answers to all these questions.

1. What does 'judo' mean?
2. How many junior grades are there?
3. What do these words mean? (a) ukemi (b) judoka (c) judogi (d) dojo (e) tatami
4. How do you submit if you are in pain?
5. What country does judo come from?
6. Why do we bow?
7. What does 'mon' mean?
8. At what age do you become a senior?
9. What is your instructor's name?
10. What is your club called?
11. Why shouldn't you chew sweets or gum on the mat?
12. How many throws can you name?
13. How many hold downs can you name?
14. What do these words mean? hajime (b) soremade (c) ippon (d) waza-ari (e) matte (f) toketa (g) osaekomi.
15. Who founded judo?
16. Who brought judo to Britain?
17. Why is it important to have short finger and toe nails?
18. Do you know three things you must not do in contests?
19. Can you tie your belt and trousers properly?
20. What grade is a yellow belt with two red tabs?
21. Why should you warm up before practice?
22. What association does your club belong to?
23. How do you score an ippon?
24. How do you score a waza-ari?
25. Why should you sit or kneel properly?
26. Why should you not talk during practice?
27. What is a judo suit called?
28. What does rei mean?
29. What was the first judo club called?
30. Who was the first non-Japanese to win a World Judo title? What nationality was he?
31. What do these initials stand for? (a) BJA (b) EJU (c) IJF.
32. What is kata-gatame?
33. What is o-goshi?
34. What signal does the referee make for ippon?
35. What signal does the referee make for waza-ari?
36. Where is the British Judo Association Head-quarters?
37. Which two types of groundwork techniques are not allowed for juniors?
38. What is the person who grades you called?
39. Who won the gold medal (under 52 kg) in the 1982 Women's World Championship?
40. What does 'tsukuri' mean?

British Judo Association Gradings

A grading is held to decide whether to promote the examinee, and if so, to which grade. The grades are shown on the belt by colour and by the number of red tabs.

Gradings are in two parts. The first part is demonstration of knowledge and skill and is usually called 'theory'. The second part consists of contests.

It is important that you learn the necessary words, throwing and hold down techniques. However good your contest results are, you cannot be promoted past your theory level.

The syllabus is reviewed every four years and is usually changed, so it is essential to have up-to-date information on what is expected.

When you prepare for your first grading, ask your instructor for a BJA individual membership application form. Send this with a postal order or cheque (never send money) to the address at the top of the form. You will receive a black record book and a membership certificate which you have to stick in the correct place in the record book.

If you look through your record book you will find the pages which cover your mon grading syllabus. This is where the examiner signs when you complete the theory part of the examination. Make sure that whoever examines you is authorised to do so. They should have a card.

Remember the membership lasts for only one year and you must apply for new membership every twelve months. You should allow three to four weeks for your new membership to be confirmed, so you must apply well before any grading or competition you want to enter, if your membership has run out.

Glossary

Chugaeri	Rolling breakfall
Dan	Black belt grade
Dojo	Judo hall
Gari	Reaping
Hajime	Begin
Ippon	Full point
Ippon-seoi-nage	Single arm shoulder throw
Jiu-jitsu	Flexible art
Judo	Flexible way
Judogi	Judo suit
Judoka	Judo person
Kake	Throw
Kami-shiho-gatame	Upper four quarters hold
Kansetsu	Armlock techniques
Kata	Pre-arranged judo techniques
Kata-gatame	Shoulder holding
Kesa-gatame	Scarf holding
Ko-soto-gari	Minor outer reaping
Ko-uchi-gari	Minor inner reaping
Kuzushi	Breaking the balance
Kyu	Learner grade
Matte	Stop
Mon	Gateway
Mune-gatame	Chest holding
O-goshi	Major hip throw
Osaekomi	Holding
O-soto-gari	Major outer reaping
O-uchi-gari	Major inner reaping
Randori	Free practice
Rei	Bow
Shiai	Contest
Shime	Strangle techniques
Sonomama	Do not move
Soremade	That is all
Tai-otoshi	Body drop
Tatami	Judo mat
Tate-shiho-gatame	Lengthwise four quarters hold
Toketa	Holding broken
Tsukuri	Getting into position for a throw
Tsuri-komi-goshi	Lifting drawing hip throw
Ukemi	Breakfall
Waza-ari	Near point
Yoko-shiho-gatame	Side four quarters hold
Yoshi	Carry on

Grading and Competition Record

Name .....S.ha.n.e..
Instructor ....
Club ....

Grading Record

GRADE	DATE	VENUE	EXAMINER	GRADE	DATE	VENUE	EXAMINER
1st MON				10th MON			
2nd MON				11th MON			
3rd MON				12th MON			
4th MON				13th MON			
5th MON				14th MON			
6th MON				15th MON			
7th MON				16th MON			
8th MON				17th MON			
9th MON				18th MON			

Competition Record

DATE	VENUE	NAME OF EVENT	WINS	LOSSES	RESULT